My Picture Book of the Planets

By Nancy E. Krulik

Scholastic Inc.
New York Toronto London Auckland Sydney

For Alison, Alex, and Lee, for whom the future is boundless.
Special thanks to Deborah Thompson for her photo research.
All photos courtesy of NASA.

Many of the photos in this book have been given false color by NASA.
Some of the pictures in this book are artist's renderings based on
information from NASA.

No part of this publication may be reproduced in whole or in
part, or stored in a retrieval system, or transmitted in any
form or by any means, electronic, mechanical, photocopying,
recording, or otherwise, without written permission of the
publisher. For information regarding permission, write to
Scholastic Inc., 730 Broadway, New York, NY 10003.

ISBN 0-590-43907-3

Copyright © 1991 by Scholastic Inc.
All rights reserved. Published by Scholastic Inc.

12 11 10 9 8 7   3 4 5 6/9

Printed in the U.S.A.   24

First Scholastic printing, January 1991

Designed by Tracy Arnold

SUN

There are nine planets in our
solar system.
They are Mercury, Venus, Earth,
Mars, Jupiter, Saturn,
Uranus, Neptune, and Pluto.
All of the planets circle around the sun.

SUN

MERCURY

Mercury is the planet closest to the sun.
It is very hot and dry.
Because it is so close to the sun,
Mercury takes the shortest amount
of time of any of the planets
to circle around the sun.

Mercury is gray, and covered
with craters.
Some of Mercury's craters are bigger
than the whole state of Texas!

Mercury's temperature is so hot, you could bake bread on the planet's surface. There is no water on Mercury.

SUN

VENUS

Venus is located closer to
Earth than any other planet.
Venus is also almost the same size
as Earth.
But Venus has no oxygen in its air,
or water on its surface,
like Earth does.

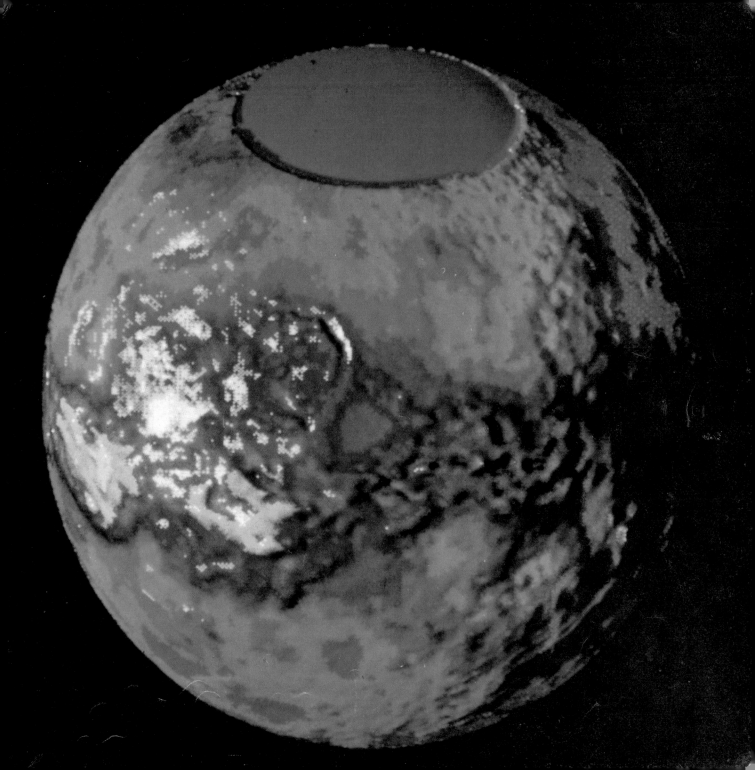

Venus is wrapped in a layer of clouds.
The clouds have a lot of sulfur in them.
The sulfur makes Venus look yellow
when we see the planet in the sky.

The clouds keep the sun's heat
from escaping.
The trapped heat makes Venus so hot,
you could melt lead on the planet's surface!

SUN

EARTH

Earth is the only planet in our solar
system to have animals and plants
living on it.
That is because Earth is the only planet
that has water.
Living things need water to survive.

SUN

MARS

Mars has the nickname the Red Planet.
That is because the sand on Mars
is made of red iron oxide.

Scientists are sure now
that there is no life on Mars.
The air surrounding Mars is too thin
to allow water to flow on the planet.
Without water, there can be no life on Mars.

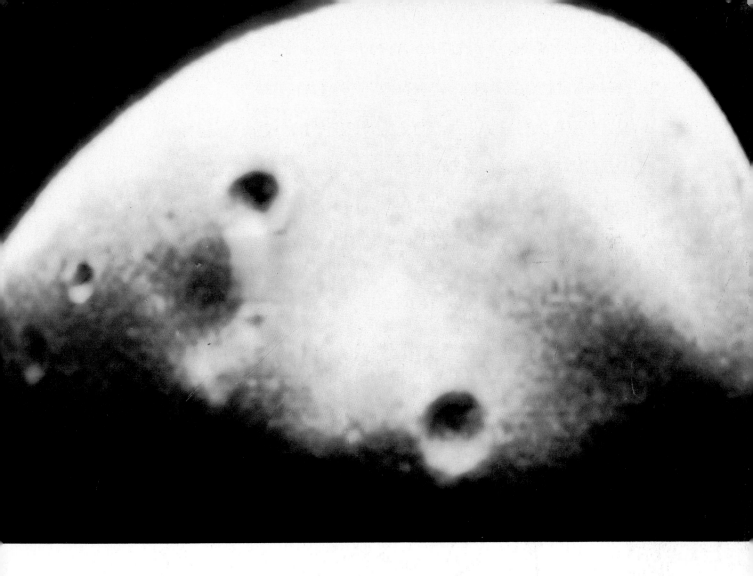

Two moons circle around Mars.
They are called Phobos and Deimos.

SUN

JUPITER

Jupiter is made almost entirely of gases.
Jupiter is best known for its
Great Red Spot.
The Great Red Spot is a swirl of gases
that is three times the size of Earth!

Jupiter is covered by a layer of clouds
that is many miles deep.
The clouds are made of chemicals
that make them appear white, red,
and brownish-red.

Thin, faint rings of ice and
dust circle around Jupiter.

SUN

SATURN

Saturn is famous for the beautiful
rings that surround it.
Its rings are made of ice, rock, and dirt.
The rings circle around the planet.

Saturn is made of gas,
just like Jupiter is.
Saturn's gases are lighter than water.
That means if you could put Saturn
into a tub of water, it would float!

Saturn is surrounded by more than 17 moons!

SUN

URANUS

Uranus is a gas planet
like Jupiter and Saturn.
It is also circled by rings.
Uranus is surrounded by gray moons.
Some scientists think there is
graphite on these moons.

Graphite is the material that pencils
are made of.

SUN

NEPTUNE

Neptune is the last planet in our
solar system that is made of gases.
It is surrounded by chunky rings.
Neptune is so far away from the sun,
it takes 165 Earth years for it to
circle all the way around the sun!

SUN

PLUTO

Pluto was the last planet to be
discovered in our solar system.
Some scientists think that Pluto
started out as one of Neptune's moons,
and then moved away from Neptune.
Pluto's moon, Charon,
is almost as big as Pluto itself!

MERCURY

VENUS

EARTH

MARS

JUPITER

SATURN

URANUS

NEPTUNE

PLUTO